Count Your Way through the
Arab World

by Jim Haskins

illustrations by Dana Gustafson

Carolrhoda Books, Inc./Minneapolis

To Elisa Beth and the future

Revised and updated edition, 1991.
Text copyright © 1987 by Jim Haskins
Illustrations copyright © 1987 by Carolrhoda Books, Inc.
Map by Laura Westlund.
Special thanks to the American-Arab
Anti-Discrimination Committee.

This book is available in two editions:
Library binding by Carolrhoda Books, Inc.
Soft cover by First Avenue Editions, 1997
c/o The Lerner Publishing Group
241 First Avenue North
Minneapolis, MN 55401 U.S.A.

LIBRARY OF CONGRESS CATALOGING-IN-PUBLICATION DATA

Haskins, James, 1941-
  Count your way through the Arab world.

  Summary: Uses Arabic numerals from one to ten to
introduce concepts about Arab countries and Arab
culture.
  1. Arab countries—Juvenile literature.   2. Arabic
language—Numerals—Juvenile literature. [1. Arab
countries.   2. Counting]   I. Gustafson, Dana, ill.
II. Title.
DS36.7.H38   1987   909'.0974927   87-6391
  ISBN 0-87614-304-4 (lib. bdg.)
  ISBN 0-87614-487-3 (pbk.)

Manufactured in the United States of America
7 8 9 10 11 12 – P/SP – 02 01 00 99 98 97

Introductory Note

Over 185 million people speak Arabic. Most of them live in the Middle East and North Africa. Written Arabic is basically the same for all of these people, but there are many different dialects (variations of speech) in spoken Arabic. This book uses the Egyptian dialect, the form of Arabic spoken in Egypt.

There are 28 letters in the Arabic alphabet, including three vowels. All other vowel sounds are shown by making small marks above and below the consonants. Arabic is written from right to left, the opposite of English. But, like English, it is read from the top of the page to the bottom.

1 (WAH-hid)

Arabic is **one** language spoken by many different peoples in the Arab world. The Arab world is not a country. It is made up of people from many countries, people who share a common language and culture. Arabs from Mauritania in Africa may not look like Arabs from Oman on the Arabian Sea, but they speak the same language. Most Arabic-speaking people live in North Africa, the Middle East, and the Arabian Peninsula. They live in countries such as Morocco, Libya, Somalia, Sudan, Saudi Arabia, Yemen, and Jordan, to name only a few. On this map, countries where Arabic is the primary or co-official language are shaded.

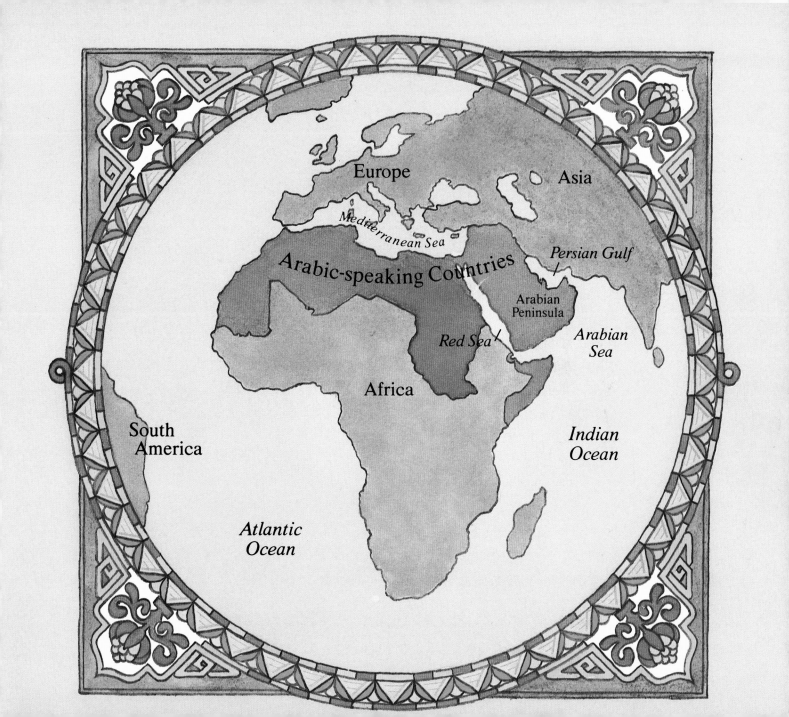

٢ 2 (it-NAYN)

Tents with **two** rooms separated by a curtain were once home to Bedouins, an Arab people who traveled and lived in the deserts of the Middle East. One of the rooms was used by the men, and the other was for the women and their possessions.

Bedouins are an independent people who were once all nomads, travelers without permanent homes. They traveled often to find grazing land for their sheep and goats and to find water for themselves. However, very few Bedouins continue to be nomadic. Most now live in one place year-round.

ﺛﻼﺛﺔ 3 (tah-LAH-tah)

"The Bird of the Golden Feather" is a folktale from Syria about **three** princes. In this tale, all three brothers search for a bird that has feathers of pure gold. Traveling together, they come upon a smooth stone on which is carved:

> This way lies the Road of the Burning
> This way lies the Road of the Drowning
> This way lies the Road of No Returning

Each prince takes a different path and each has many adventures.

There are hundreds of Arab folktales. Many of them begin with these words: "This happened, or maybe it did not. The time is long past, and much is forgot."

ع **4** (ar-BAH-ah)

When we think of a family, we often picture a mother, father, and children. In traditional Arab households, as many as **four** generations of one family lived together. Children, their parents, grandparents, and any living great-grandparents shared one house or several houses grouped around a courtyard.

Nowadays, fewer Arabs live in "extended" families, but cousins, aunts and uncles, and grandparents often live nearby. With so many relatives around, children get a lot of attention. Family members carefully watch children to keep them safe and protected and to make sure they behave themselves. This support system has always been the major strength of Arab families.

5

△ (KAHM-sah)

Many Arabic-speaking people live in countries outside the Arab world. Some show pride in their culture by wearing traditional clothing. Others practice a traditional religion.

Most Arabs of the Muslim religion pray **five** times a day. When they pray, they must always face toward Mecca, the holy city in Saudi Arabia. In this way, the faithful are able to remember God—Allah in Arabic—and their homeland, no matter where they live.

Nearly nine in ten Arabs are Muslims, or members of the religion of Islam. Muslims worship Allah and follow the teachings of the prophet Muhammad. Muslims believe that Muhammad, who was born about A.D. 570, was Allah's messenger. Muslims remember Allah and Muhammad's teachings in their prayers, whether they are merchants in London, engineers in China, teachers in the United States, workers in France, or students in Moscow.

٤6 (SIHT-tah)

There are **six** major ways of traveling in the Arab world. Animals, such as camels and mules, used to be the most common way of getting people and goods across the mountains and deserts of North Africa, the Middle East, and the Arabian Peninsula. Camels are native to the Arab world and provided milk, meat, hides

for making tents and clothing, and transportation. In modern times, camels are being replaced by other kinds of transportation. Nowadays, Arabs travel by car, bus, truck, train, airplane—and sometimes still on a camel's back.

∨ **7** **(SAHB-ah)**

The Koran, the holy book of Islam, states that all Muslims who can afford to must make a pilgrimage—or Hajj in Arabic—to the city of Mecca, in Saudi Arabia. They must go at least once in their lifetime.

Once in Mecca, Muslims circle the Kaaba **seven** times. The Kaaba is the holiest shrine of Islam. The Black Stone within the Kaaba's walls is believed to be part of the original shrine built by the prophet Abraham thousands of years ago.

∧ 8 (ta-MAHN-ya)

In Arabic, there are **eight** different ways to say cousin. Each way describes the exact relationship of that person to his or her family. A male cousin, then, can be introduced in one of four different ways:

ibn AHMM
father's brother's son

ibn AHMM-eh
father's sister's son

ibn KHAL
mother's brother's son

ibn KHAL-eh
mother's sister's son

A female cousin can also be introduced in one of four different ways:

bent AHMM
  father's brother's daughter

bent AHMM-eh
  father's sister's daughter

bent KHAL
  mother's brother's daughter

bent KHAL-eh
  mother's sister's daughter

Arabs have been known as traders for nearly 3,000 years. The Arab world exports **nine** major products: oil, natural gas, petroleum products, phosphates, fertilizers, dates, olives, olive oil, and cotton cloth. In Arab countries, people buy and sell goods in shops and outdoor markets.

Local markets in the Arab world are full of color from displays of (1) cloth, (2) embroidery, and (3) rugs; smells from (4) spices, (5) tea, and (6) coffee; and good-tasting food from the stands of (7) greengrocers, (8) dried fruit merchants, and (9) butchers.

١. 10 (AH-shah-rah)

Sand dunes in the Arab world are huge hills of sand that can extend for as many as **ten** miles.

While much of the Arab world is desert, it is also known for its mountains, river valleys, and coastlines. Many Arabs live in farm country along the Nile in Egypt and Sudan, by the Euphrates and Tigris rivers in Iraq and Syria, and on the southern Mediterranean coast in Morocco, Algeria, Tunisia, and Libya.